The Writings of 2-14-26

Michael D. Jones

ISBN: 0692947752
ISBN 13: **9780692947753**

When we look at unity and division,

We see a picture not clearly painted.

We see a segment of reality that

Depicts a source of creative works.

I'm picturing chance; you

See, its chance that defines

Potential and its unity and

Division that arise as an opportunity

To chance our potential as the source of value.

Being who you are, you are capable

Of anything, but it's because we're divided that anything is left to

Chance. If our circumstance defines our

Potential, then our opportunity

To value unity is divided, because

Mere division is circumstance

That hasn't been unified by the common bond of chance.

<u>1–19</u>

Close your eyes, and picture a place; on this journey you won't need a face.

If you calculate failures, you fail or limit losses. So limiting

Losses take focus from success, so as to say,

"Success doesn't just define itself as failures in their totality."

Untitled

I think, but I see a mirror.

<u>December 10, 2010</u>

<u>6:03 a.m.</u>

Our means of presence to the deferment of natural means is an effect
to show

What would have occurred.

<u>December 17, 2010</u>

<u>11:20 p.m.</u>

I believe selective prospect has been an enabling vexation because

Judgment

Up to this point has been valued as that of reality.

<u>12:05 a.m.</u>

To depict the limitless has limited its being; you differentiate the

Overall strategy of its measure. Then it's possible to cultivate its

Skills in exercising its being. Patience is being, so it's depleted due

To this circumstance, but the fruit of that self-image is patience so

That limiting has its remedies in that method.

We turn practically to granulate makeup within our own existence.

My first glimpse of wisdom was one in vengeance, but with my

heart, I've embraced the likelihood of being the threat of difference.

Abstract

You open waters upon the confuted pressed-reality changes.

UNTITLED

December 6, 2010—6:06 a.m.

I'm the angel that couldn't fly,

The one wouldn't die,

The eyes that wouldn't cry,

And the hearth you couldn't buy.

You see, my pain is my light

While I strain to fight in the dark

Under what remains as some opponents hark,

A hark to my heart kindled in their dark.

Lessened by the cry of pain,

I can't deny or shame the possibility that insight is the furthest from

Light's day. So see my form is as warm as your homes shapeless

Born. When I could fly and see the sky is too high.

Bars and Walls

Along the road is clearly a milestone

Outside a house in order.

Identity!

Let's expose and imagine dominion

To introduce a nature of natural means to create a sense to analyze.

Wayward feelings of facts

Hurt those immune to the held bond of intra I Sight.

Although theirs an theirs of grander and the blood on the hands of

The lost,

Fear man is deceitful; generations of cursed and torn hearts close

Walls to break.

So close to walls broken, passion does not reach to walls perverted.

<u>Untitled</u>

Wisdom is drawn out of society's similarities and derives in our differences.

1:15 a.m.

Arms extend, but eyes close. Emotions connect, but blinds close.

Do pleasure and pain equal the works of aether and ether, at hands of

Work?

Do we take care so or comprehend difficulty regretted: rule, order,

And benefit from the universe above?

<u>Untitled</u>

Although ideas are opportunities given willingly, pursue it in

appearance by an application of difference.

What earthly heaven should allow free will? Continuous will and will alone shall free us from this fearless place.

Fearful Eyes

I'm a poet, which in one disguise

Attains by a Portuguese surprise

Literal insignia of a hero from an art of love.

It is an instance in which we emerge from pain

Disguised in the darkness, as one hated would hear,

Not distinguished from this fire.

Look to this shame balanced from love and despair's desire.

It is breaking down the love that delivers still the balance in the

Midst.

I've quit and trusted to rid one's self of this lusted fear.

Toll Park

Very seldom are the different songs of sung deeds by themselves intuition. Solutions render gray these tolls as the day's old ticket to a morbid song.

<u>Untitled</u>

<u>March 3, 2011</u>

I, You, Me, US—next to the sticker that says hence, "I've read, I think, I listen, so benefit."

O Africa

Closed doors, footsteps, echoing snug in the river that is.

Choosing to close the rivers' powerless doors, rescue us from our

Fresh start.

The sky has met the rivers blue and limited its queue.

With this groove, it's just that we've ourselves found in lieu

Love

Love

Love

Spare this reality to me.

Untitled

May 21, 2011

The cynical states of the union,

The pinnacle of delusion,

The choice of seclusion…

Aren't we all in peril?

Or are we all in a carol?

Input those who have risen?

Having character's recluse in our midst, in this love

Purges the wine to drink as the love, as worry clearly reasons too.

As it's asking, haven't we come to the conclusion

That the ration of the earth is in ruin?

The more accomplished see no less, but the proactive

Have flown from the nest.

Depression has sat in, and consideration invented has crept to the

Depth

Far beyond the levels of steps below lewdness.

<u>May 21</u>

<u>The Sickness of Youth</u>

The elastic currency of an elastic youth is set to turn.

At the turning, days are prettier days ahead as

Gray like a cloak of mutual understating that has faded way.

Are our youth our watchers, pure in intellect and loved reminders?

Untitled

Clear thoughts of me and you are this vivid and abundant radiance

From the sky's blues as it's erased to shut truths.

I know it's you, sunny where there's more to do.

Like the sound of love and its means forever yours.

Closed doors of the shoes washing the pure-white sands.

Differences are at hand,

And even though I should, it'll lend me a hand.

Hearth felt by it mend, behaving is in interest never lost scaring the

Pavement sand.

With dark signs across, our stares undreamed by time closed by the

Shores we define.

It would never, even in the madness, be believed as two, but as love

New.

Me

Life's ups have really bottomed out.

Clearly this bottom is my route.

I'm merely doubted as a hum

Here at the bottom.

Dancing and acknowledged by the forgotten,

We bump heads to let them graze this chest as fear self-indulged to

Rest.

I am alone here at the forsaken bottom and can't fin.

Attested and rested unless my light shines within.

I will stay here awhile with ambitions of a child, as it's too much all

To know.

Which harkens now as the dark, and so the might I might muster

Here at the bottom intergraded alone, I can reach no height.

<u>Brand</u>

<u>December 20, 2011</u>

The logic behind my pain is simple:

Choose your battle, and reprehend them for scars and mistakes.

Close to a god it is what a voice and meek psalm take.

I am obsolete. The media says this,

Men pure in intellect say, A being exists; nonetheless, I'm being

As much to any days where this colder

Dish and insist says that walls don't exist.

I am much overborne because seasons have passed.

Each shoulder seemingly surpassed its wisdom and each backlash.

So at the close, the night out from a picture not plainly seen.

I hope in vain while praying to this dream.

February 8, 2012

I am advocate to the sky,

Like the blue bird that flies.

I am a ripple in the ocean,

A whole to infinite motion.

My love is aquatinted with

The lonely heart and morally believed as

Faint rights are the shreds solely

Shred for soles worn like threads upon these frozen, dark skin cloths

That meet at night.

Dark hearts have come to light,

Each in the shadow of our sight.

My life has been in vain, but this is only because I've experienced

Pain. How has thy heart not been affected?

When the only vanity is rain, it drips from our eyes and stains each

Loving gain.

Math

The idea is old,

Like the fire chews coals.

The truth is a mold.

Now, how and how old?

I've confined myself to these walls,

Left open like the firm's faith for calls.

That we are ready in all.

Now, we're formal.

This presence is new in forming a new fright from me to you,

Wrapped in colors set for two.

I am me, and you are you; this is true, as we are

Two plus two.

4-22-12

Cold Shoulders

The time I spend

Twined and bent

Is just the end of love mended.

Lessen the greater burden of life because

The days it rains are cold and plain

When they come across vain.

Only now do I stand

Just as a child is balanced in

A world of the invisible hands.

Incite a simile, and blame what's

Meant to hold every memory.

Grown, we'd know this mend's every hug.

Desolate bosoms

Closed doors tearing

At the permanent peace

Of listening to menials sticking,

We are preparing to meet.

Opportunity is where

Closed meetings propose

The list of topics; to be specific, these

Teachings are closed.

Or hasn't the sky turned red?

Under the blanket of conversation,

Where the earth and waters have met,

Clouded by judgment of the finer wave

Of radial responsibility to those who have been made to engrave?

Juggle the responsibility of the sonic youth.

Have we met before?

Due to closed doors jarred up

By the anklet of the

Past chains, barred up by the families

Of the sea to know that the

Ocean is vast like he.

It's still said truth's third sabbatical is the second year of faith,

Parentally parted to conditioning

Endurance at the race.

Ideal Arms

You see, elegance is my worst enemy.

It gets into me. Word to the king:

Inside the pit it's occupied

By rights and rings that tour the fingers' whys!

Outlets gone as the song of the barren.

A woman is left alone to the pale moon,

Consumed by the night's gale and room.

I know my mouth allows the deserted reformation to conclude

Individual duality; blessed and instead of just the rights,

I regarded life too. Conscious birth of a child's

Heights, mild, moderate blues. This ministered child!

Our concise silence walks the mile but up the upright altar

Of the superficial as it's making a marquis a miraculous nursery

Rhyme.

Still, the second year as the responsibility to

Constitute a mess and remedy as the intimacy and worth. The *odds*

Of favor of the worst gods instate loss.

A loss of mind in an asylum generation given perdition has

Impressed confidence and

Adders in wisdoms and choose in turn this.

In time walk; the line and the cure the idioms we learn.

Still we earn

Still we earn

Still we earn

Still we earn

The desolate mind has found its place with the regard

Of the world as a time to waste. The desolate mind's place

Ought to reach greater accomplishments in regard of the line of

Lines, clinched, and find that perfections are in minds of ideal arms

In lies.

Fifth Day

Hilled visions of death,

Success chilled by tears wept.

What percentage calls this home?

Death is as an interesting step aside; ideas creative to get those

Regrets together so don't look back.

The null left the epoch thickened, stiffened, and shared by freedom

And envy.

Showing love is the stencil outlined and penciled.

Interesting issue,

Like how the news sees an

Obituary of a man with no bio—

Just for them indeed.

They've been unified to know that

Factors in a factor assure reliability.

Usually counts range from fallacies' and plasticity's

Indexed ingresses cited by the physical analyses indecencies.

Is an Aster 9 a catalyst to bring malice in?

Are nickel-plated hearts designed to bring in the words, hence

Success as a birth?

That calls for a birth, given that psychometrics are instruments.

Be ye a piece with no element to send from it us,

Heaven timid amid waiting, as leading and sinning

Are concurrent censorships from that with which the instrument

On the fifth day follows as an intern, showing intervention permits

No mention.

Who

My passion is too masked, upon the demolishing injustice worldwide by means of creative business ventures, focusing through the legal run on both primary and secondary existence.

Take the treat out of the process to create the phoneme.

Picture these

Who are they, and how best can we reach them? It's enough to picture when stated. Some things are built as external rewards that will discern this question; I know this myself. Take for instance aliens, who are they? Better yet, how best can we introduce Earth to them? Honestly, but who believes in aliens any more than the liberating angels? Let me be a little more specific; I've changed listens, it gives us a branch on a matter that's down, never up, as it's longing introduction is responding in language ascertainable, doubting governing experience as unalike!

Different time zones speak for everyone; let's just know the matters are relevantly lacking too. As for the alien above, we've labeled those social intercourses in humanity, via greater character, as the very best never sought.   Are we thoroughly alive? Well, there are certain feelings toward the good things in life that can't be replaced morbid though for one unlike; two different for any error; and three, for keeping up with the head on our shoulders to break tide with peace. Mysteries are broken down, and the love is. Every problem is the best solution for differences. If every problem looks like a nail, then we may as well buy plenty of hammers, so as to say

our space of difference is like painting a picture not clearly seen and

not having the right colors to group.

I

I'm going to illustrate a place where we

Educate business in the sphere to have influence

At different interfaces. Remember, in time we move with haste.

When you show up, he shows up but reflects the waste is his taste.

Tongues are the revelation and gratification of the royal flush

Attitude.

In magnitude of our choice, but so people with full potential would

Define us as turning truth to the world, but no longer will for my

Identity. Could we define a world missing pieces, licenses, and

Fences? A "road mentally realized" as Armageddon essentially

Renders burning desire with a fire.

Let's be as ambiguous as a nobleman to receive soup.

Could we bear the height the fence?

A strategy of preeminence, since this is true:

The rivers don't want to move.

The Longest Minute

Time moves forward right.

Have my years been toward right?

Do I grow wise and gray?

And careful because my thoughts

Have dismayed my youth's ways

Of siding courage at bay?

The answer is "No, see, the

World is my puzzle." Slowly

I piece the rubble from a picture too divided, revived of

Corruption and sheaved like my pieces that deviate

Each meaning as gum and gumption.

I erupt and yet pulse for my completion

And pieces of devotion, for now I am broke because

Each image is mine won.

I am.

5-5

A poet's eyes are ones that

Stay open. I've dived in the depths of solitude to collude

There, cured and set for beauty.

I truly pass by in ye eyes just to say hey.

So indirect and erect, with clearly

No place to be. Judged free and rushed thee to see

The protruding eyes.

These brown eyes. I have

Seen by the days and a way

So old that critical judgment pays a role.

Not gold or paper.

Buy Me a Decision

Cast out all doubt,

Face-to-face,

Mouth to mouth,

The chase in this race.

Tell me—do you believe?

Have we induced what we conceive?

At first glance in our stance,

We've tamed this chance.

Under this spell, lust or sunk

Refrain, but stay blessed.

Continue on—you sail;

The tide does share its own as its own idea,

Alone prone to rise above the brix and flow out each continuum.

Truth

Honest intellect,

Dishonest faith.

I'm aided by passion and grace;

I've lost my taste.

Let's not talk of words or things;

Let's share intangible love.

Mock each stare

That fared by this drug.

I mean no harm, just a felling fared from what I will to bear;

Understand I'm rare

I know that healing it curses what we share.

So passion and love spare me nothing above my commitment;

We couldn't truthfully muster up to it.

Life

The turns on the road come together;

The stresses of life last forever.

Should I be here, or will things change?

Aren't my highs in life outlets?

To me? Well, I pardon those who wait silent,

Their jargon hardened sands as my lips defiant.

You see in here, but just reliant

On the resentful airs

That you are tyrants.

Silently they count many steps and mistakes,

Each a take to circumcise my fate.

Here on the road is the phase I mention is my fate.

These Expressions

How do you rarely come together

Whenever this world is in need?

How hasn't the early bee eaten what she needs?

We borrow, we steal all to just heal and kill, and today the seal has

Been filed. The seal of expressions, desire,

Digressions, fire loosely tighten into this depression.

It's become first thought of expression and its dire constraint that

This cold, bitter bite of the revolving date between trusts uses

Confession. Who says no more, for we've reached stalemate with

Our fates?

The coward knows no honor;

I refuse to sponsor this courage.

What fact shows strength?

When a coward's courage is missing,

Do we gather around to see the hero

Who is selfless and zeroed in

On his role from the beginning?

One begets the other's energy,

Yet their mirrors say we

Connect when our job is not done yet.

"See, you rescued me from the desolate," says the coward.

"I was asleep," says the hero.

Both agree one is asleep,

Walking, and not quite

Aware of their consciousness.

So for the hero who knows not depth is at rest,

Let him live though external rest,

And the coward waits in a knot.

Will he find what's missing from the identity of both?

Indefinitely the bond that a hero and a coward share is knotty, as

They'd know once tested.

Now, for them who have this, man be a part in both the ways to rise

And show his reality is what the totality

Of listlessness brings, for the hero and coward proved we'd be slow

In advancing, a day when we will be more than a man and his hero.

Don't Get Left Behind

So there's this place, and it's mine. There's something about it that makes our existence dwell in its most uninspired times. This place is where intellects meet and the sport of life is illustrated in a picture not clearly painted. Down the funnel in this place is a mix of fern of assertive and honest dealing. So much so there are two reasons to go. One is to limit the picture of pain, and the other is to mirror this fantasy we call limelight. The mind's mirror has clearly met its hall, and through this great place, the normalcy is beyond a set of shoes or a nice suit. The music bumps, and the people lurk one at a time until the clock reads dirt.

The shudder of the small room is a place where the adults celebrate and a place where boys become men and girls become women. There are people see you every day, and the location is never different, but life is easy as you mean. There are night gals and night owls in threads never seen; inside each thread are the hearts of what we guess. Our grounds derive from our similarities, so here there are no differences—just the draws out of society. "The issues of the masses are pure," said the man of intellect.

We all say he's crazy because there are just issues in the masses. "We are filled with tremendous motives," the man of class said. Great words in the world of the know, but in the world here they are questionable—as is illustrated in its finest hour. Here at the hour of the perfection is the delight of the crowd, and the games of the boastful are games of the night. The night comes to an end as the people gaze at each other with frigid looks upon their faces as sweat pours down the brows. The planning and listening have captured the hearts and extended their choices to those aspects I consider first resolutions. Fiction, nonfiction, and clear deeds of the wholehearted—only just a few have departed. How haven't we come here before when the only thing in this place and across the street is the depression of a familiar tone on the phone with the anxiety of former access to this place?

Tomorrow hasn't come, but now the powerless run by the short-tempered man; the sound boys of the night have clouded and taken from them as the input in the car creates policy. The only thing more important than this place in this time is the density of the night. Now here people have met the night density of black t's and 2:45 a.m., and the night has ended with the fern, but due to the permissions, the moon settled at one. Its 2:50 a.m. now and there are better things to do while merely the reputation is what we think. Ten minutes later people are doing what's right as a reminder of what's right.

Although profits, conscience decree, and thought outlets cause this splendor, it's laughter. What do we all have in common counts? If you ask me, I would weep and never tell. So I ask a friend, and tell me, "One may say it, but another day I won't; it's not a decision for me." OK, so I ask another friend, and he tells me, "I haven't even heard of those places, so I can't make the question just easier by the way you take it." Lastly, I go to the only friend I know, and he says, "I will tell you only when you're willing for it to happen." Now, at first there were ways to agree with these conclusions at night, since I did more investigation into the actual definition of "right." The first person told me, "One may say it, but another day because I won't; it's not a decision for me." I go to the local store and ask the cashier if he knows exactly what this is supposed to mean.

He gives me a blank look, as though we only have the habit of breathing over the phone. Stunned, I repeat the response, and he says, "That's the first person." Now I have gotten somewhere. I begin to make these progressions in seeing and choosing my destiny, but none of these understandings seems to make any sense. I leave the store and proceed across the crosswalk to turn into the next store to find out who in the world has an answer for my questions.

"Encumbered by profit, I see!" a woman yells.

"Yes!" I yell back. She motions at me and asks me to give her a reason she shouldn't charge me for the answer. "Answer, please; you saw my shirt, and yes, it does say profit!" I tell her to button that smile and continue to go about my way.

As I make the decision to finally put these things together, I come up with these closed doors, but keep the window locked. Profit, decree, and thought outlets. Hmm, it's like closing the door for a woman. Then it occurs to me I will not get paid till the next week; why am I wasting time walking when I drive to surpass how questions always answer that? This outlet ought to turn over their time too. I last as long as life's energy.

Short Trip

Choices extended by an integrated heart,

Voices concise to the silent dark.

"How are you? Does the sky fall?

Or does conscientious silence short talk?"

Determine us, as much as we determine everything.

"We earn lust just like we earn trust."

Trustworthy buzz of the present ceased to communicate.

"Blow the rest away; commune precious moments." Slumbers

Hushed.

Hope fades through teaching or graze learning,

"Secular leaning in a countless haze earning;

Discerning, yearning desire of an equate,

And I can more make it prodigal, as you've seen."

Marred, now just replace desolate haste with the unification,

Here then by this race where the short trip is transparent but clear.

www.ingramcontent.com/pod-product-compliance
Lightning Source LLC
LaVergne TN
LVHW010031070426
835508LV00005B/297